Table Content

1. Acknowledgement
2. Topic clarification
3. Character profiles
4. Themes and analysis

Acknowledgment

I would like to extend my heartfelt gratitude to those who have made this story possible.

Firstly, a special thank you to Khalushi Frans, my dedicated and hardworking author. Your unwavering commitment, creativity, and passion have breathed life into this story. Your vision and perseverance are the foundation of this work, and without your determination, this story would not have come to fruition.

A big thank you also goes to Gift Sambo, for your meticulous work in proofreading and editing. Your attention to detail and invaluable input have ensured that this story shines with clarity and precision. Your patience and expertise have elevated this narrative, and I am deeply grateful for your contribution.

To my family, friends, and readers, I am incredibly thankful for your continued support and encouragement. This journey would not be the same without each and every one of you.

This book is not just a product of one person's effort, but a collective collaboration of those who believe in the power of storytelling. Thank you all for being a part of this journey

With gratitude

Thambo Sifiso

Topic Clarification for "The Forbidden Waters: Magic, Love, and Family Ties"

1. **The Forbidden Waters**:

- This refers to the river, which plays a central role in the story. The waters are "forbidden" due to the supernatural and cursed nature of the river, symbolizing danger, mystery, and a place where boundaries between the mortal world and the supernatural are thin. The river is off-limits due to the curses, the magic it holds, and the consequences of tampering with it. It also reflects the forbidden relationships, like that of Zandile and Frans, and the tragic consequences of pursuing them.

2. **Magic**:

    - Magic is a fundamental element in the story, both literally and metaphorically. The river's enchantment and the mystical powers of characters like Laura (the river queen) show how magic shapes the lives of those involved. The theme of magic isn't just about supernatural powers; it's also about how individuals' actions, relationships, and desires can have magical, life-altering consequences. It's also about the transformation of characters as they interact with the mystical aspects of the world.

3. **Love**:

    - Love is another driving force in the narrative. The relationships between Frans and the

Mkhize sisters (Zandile and Sibongile), as well as the complicated dynamics in the family, are influenced by love, desire, and betrayal. These emotions often conflict with the moral codes set by their families and the supernatural rules of the river. The forbidden love between Frans and Zandile, in particular, sets in motion the chain of events that lead to the ultimate tragedy and redemption.

4. **Family Ties**:
    - Family is a critical theme in the story, particularly the Mkhize family's curse, which is tied to their ancestors and the river. The family dynamics, especially the relationship between Mrs. Mkhize and her daughters, and the influence of ancestral curses, highlight how family bonds are both a source of strength and a curse in themselves. The Mkhize family's traditions, their rigid control over their daughters, and the mother's vengeful actions reflect the complex ways family ties influence individual choices and outcomes.

Character clarification

1. Frans Justin

- **Role:** The protagonist of the story, Frans is a young man who struggles with his past and desires redemption. His journey is one of transformation, as he grapples with forbidden love, betrayal, and a chance for redemption through supernatural intervention.

- **Personality:** Frans is conflicted, torn between his emotions and moral compass. His desires often lead him to make mistakes, but he ultimately seeks redemption. He is vulnerable yet strong, showing his ability to learn and grow, especially through the guidance of Mr. Zondi and his experiences with the river queen.

2. Zandile Mkhize

- **Role:** Zandile is one of the Mkhize sisters, and her love for Frans is a central plot point in the story. She is caught between her family's expectations and her love for Frans, creating a deep emotional conflict within her. However, her relationship with Frans is disrupted by her mother's manipulations.

- **Personality:** Zandile is kind-hearted and loving but struggles with the pressure from her mother and the rules of her family. She is innocent but eventually learns the complexities of love and loyalty. Her love for Frans drives much of the story, and her eventual grounding by her mother highlights the consequences of her emotions.

3. Sibongile Mkhize

- **Role:** Sibongile is another sister in the Mkhize family, and she plays a significant role in manipulating Frans. She pretends to have romantic feelings for him, ultimately leading him astray in a complex plot of deception and betrayal.

- **Personality:** Sibongile is cunning and manipulative, using her charm to deceive Frans into believing she is the one meant for him. She is determined and takes advantage of the power her family holds over her. Her actions demonstrate how deceit and personal desires can lead to dangerous consequences.

4. Mrs. Mkhize

- **Role:** Mrs. Mkhize, the mother of Zandile and Sibongile, is a controlling and manipulative figure. She plays a key role in driving the story's tension by enforcing her family's traditional beliefs and using her daughters to manipulate Frans. She also represents the darker side of tradition and familial duty.

- **Personality:** Mrs. Mkhize is authoritarian, and her manipulative nature drives the plot's conflicts. She is willing to go to extreme lengths to maintain control over her daughters, even going so far as to threaten Frans's life. Her actions represent the consequences of blind loyalty to tradition and the destructiveness of unchecked power.

5. Laura (The River Queen)

- Role: Laura, also known as the river queen, is a mystical and supernatural being who represents magic and redemption in the story. She helps Frans by offering him a chance to redeem himself from his past sins, and she is an essential figure in the narrative's exploration of forgiveness and transformation.

- Personality: Laura is enigmatic, wise, and otherworldly. She embodies the idea of mercy and transformation. While she is kind and nurturing to the boys, she also has the power to enforce justice when necessary, as seen with the tragic end of the Mkhize sisters. Laura's actions are driven by a greater purpose, seeking to balance the forces of nature and morality.

6. Mr. Zondi

- **Role:** Mr. Zondi is a mentor and father figure to Frans. He adopts Frans after recognizing the boy's troubled path and guides him toward a better life. Mr. Zondi is the moral anchor in the story, offering wisdom and support to Frans when he is lost.

- **Personality:** Mr. Zondi is wise, patient, and compassionate. He sees potential in Frans and serves as a voice of reason throughout the story. His role as an adoptive father highlights themes of redemption, second chances, and the importance of mentorship.

7. The Mkhize Sisters (Collectively)

- **Role:** The Mkhize sisters, Zandile and Sibongile, represent the traditional expectations placed on young women in their community. They are the subjects of their mother's control and reflect the complexity of familial duty, loyalty, and rebellion. Their lives and actions are shaped by their mother's influence, which ultimately leads to their downfall.

- **Personality:** While Zandile is more innocent and loving, Sibongile is more cunning and manipulative. Both sisters are shaped by the love and pressure they feel from their mother. Their lives intertwine with the supernatural world, where their fates are sealed due to their actions.

8. The Dogs

- Role: The dogs are a symbolic force of nature that act as a manifestation of retribution. They are tied to the theme of justice, attacking Frans as a consequence of his actions. The appearance of the dogs marks a turning point in Frans's journey, reinforcing the consequences of his past behavior.

- **Personality:** The dogs are fierce, aggressive, and uncontrollable, embodying the idea of nature's power to enforce justice. Their role in chasing Frans represents the inescapable consequences of one's actions and the punishment that follows.

9. The Ghost

- **Role:** After death, the ghost become vengeful forces, terrorizing the village. Their presence ties into the supernatural elements of the story and the theme of retribution.

- **Personality:** The ghost are vengeful and angry, representing the unresolved emotional turmoil and consequences of the bad peoples actions. Their haunting presence serves as a warning about the costs of betrayal, manipulation, and dishonesty.

10. Bongeni

- **Role**: Bongeni is a close friend of Frans and one of his companions in the adventure. While not central to the main conflict, Bongeni plays a supportive role in the story. He is part of the group of boys who go on the camping trip by the river and is involved in the discovery of the river queen, Laura. Bongeni represents loyalty and friendship, providing a contrast to the more dramatic and conflicted characters like Frans and the Mkhize sisters.

- **Personality**: Bongeni is friendly, good-natured, and practical. He enjoys life and adventure but has a more grounded approach to situations. His presence in the story offers light-heartedness and camaraderie. Bongani's unwavering loyalty to his friends helps them navigate the dangers they face and makes him a valuable companion on their journey.

11. Sifiso

- **Role**: Sifiso is another of Frans's friends, also involved in the camping trip and the events at the river. Like Bongeni, he adds to the sense of camaraderie and adventure in the story. Sifiso is more observant and strategic, often serving as the voice of reason when things get intense. While he doesn't always act in the same way as Frans, he plays a role in helping the group understand the situation with the river queen and the treasure.

- **Personality**: Sifiso is intelligent, calm under pressure, and thoughtful. He tends to analyse situations and make decisions based on logic rather than emotions. His ability to stay grounded in the midst of supernatural occurrences allows him to help his friends make sense of the mysteries around them. Sifiso's role is key in encouraging Frans to consider the long-term consequences of his actions, particularly when it comes to the supernatural world and the danger that comes with it.

THEMES

1. Redemption and Forgiveness

- **Explanation**: The central theme of redemption in the story revolves around the protagonist, Frans, seeking absolution for his past sins. The river queen, Laura, offers him a chance to cleanse himself of guilt, symbolizing the idea that individuals can find forgiveness and transformation, even when they feel lost or trapped in their past mistakes.
- **Key Elements**: Frans's journey of redemption is marked by his encounter with the river queen, who helps him reconcile with his past. The supernatural element of the river queen's mercy serves as a metaphor for the possibility of change, showing that no matter how deep one's sins are, there is always a chance for atonement.

2. Supernatural Influence and Magic

- **Explanation**: This theme is expressed through the presence of the river queen and the magical elements in the story. The river, with its powers to heal or curse, becomes a key part of the narrative, influencing the characters' fates and decisions. The mermaids and the appearance of the magical box full of treasure signify the blend of the mystical with reality.
- **Key Elements**: The river queen's true identity as a supernatural being, the magical powers she possesses, and the impact of these powers on the mortal world are crucial. These elements are tied to

ancient myths and magic that shape the lives of those involved.

3. Love and Desire

- **Explanation**: Love, in both its pure and forbidden forms, is a central theme in the story. The attraction between Frans and the Mkhize sisters, especially his emotional entanglement with Zandile, explores themes of lust, desire, and the consequences of pursuing such feelings against societal or moral boundaries.

- **Key Elements**: The love triangle involving Frans, Zandile, and Sibongile illustrates the tension between romantic desire and the limitations imposed by family, society, and personal responsibility. The attraction is complicated by the supernatural elements and the moral dilemmas each character faces.

4. Betrayal and Deception

- **Explanation**: Several characters in the story engage in betrayal and deception, particularly Mrs. Mkhize and Sibongile. Mrs. Mkhize uses her influence over her daughters to control their choices and deceive them about the consequences of their actions. Sibongile's attempts to manipulate Frans show how deceit can drive the characters to dangerous situations.

- **Key Elements**: The lies told by Mrs. Mkhize and the manipulation of Frans by Sibongile are key examples of this theme. The deception surrounding Laura's identity as the river queen also adds to the sense of betrayal, as Frans is unaware of the true nature of his interaction with her.

5. Family and Loyalty

- **Explanation**: The concept of family loyalty and duty plays a significant role in the narrative. The Mkhize sisters' loyalty to their mother, despite her cruel demands, contrasts with Frans's loyalty to his friends and his eventual bond with Mr. Zondi, who becomes a father figure after seeing Frans's troubled life.

- **Key Elements**: The tension between personal desires and familial obligations is seen when Zandile is forced to choose between her love for Frans and her loyalty to her mother's wishes. Frans's decision to adopt Mr. Zondi's guidance is a turning point in the story, symbolizing the importance of finding a new family when the old one fails to support.

6. Moral Consequences

- **Explanation**: The characters' actions, whether good or bad, come with moral consequences. The story demonstrates that choices made in the heat of passion, betrayal, or greed have lasting effects, and the consequences are often more profound than anticipated.

- **Key Elements**: Frans's encounter with the river queen and the subsequent impact on his life reflect the theme of moral consequence. Mrs. Mkhize and the tragic end of the Mkhize sisters also serve as a cautionary tale about the price of dishonesty and manipulation.

7. The Power of Nature

- **Explanation**: The river, as a natural force, represents the unstoppable flow of fate and destiny. It is a force that shapes the lives of the characters, from offering a path to redemption to providing the gold that changes the fortunes of the Zondi family. The river symbolizes both creation and destruction.

- **Key Elements**: The river's ability to both heal and harm is central to the plot. Its role in cleansing Frans's sins and in bringing about the downfall of the Mkhize family highlights the dual nature of nature's power.

8. Cultural Beliefs and Traditions

- **Explanation**: The story includes elements of African folklore, magic, and cultural practices, particularly around the Mkhize family's traditions and their beliefs in ancestral power and family hierarchy. These cultural elements influence the characters' actions and decisions throughout the story.

- **Key Elements**: The Mkhize family's customs, such as the first-born rule, and the supernatural beliefs around the river queen are key cultural aspects that shape the characters' motivations. The story shows how cultural expectations can drive people to act in ways that are not always morally right.

9. Wealth and Greed

- **Explanation**: The theme of wealth and its impact on human nature is explored through the treasure found in the river. Greed, desire for power, and the pursuit of riches are shown to motivate some of the characters, leading them down dangerous paths. However, wealth also brings redemption, symbolizing the complex relationship between materialism and morality.

- **Key Elements**: The gold, silver, and diamonds symbolize both the lure of material wealth and its potential to corrupt. Frans's acquisition of the treasure from the river represents both a reward and a burden.

10. Justice and Retribution

- **Explanation**: The idea of divine or natural justice is represented through the tragic end of the Mkhize sisters, who are punished for their deceit and cruelty.

The river queen serves as an agent of retribution, ensuring that those who act maliciously face consequences, whether it be through death or supernatural intervention.

- **Key Elements**: Mrs. Mkhize's manipulative actions lead to her downfall, and the river's vengeance upon her daughters highlights the theme of justice. The idea that actions, both good and bad, are always met with corresponding consequences is central to this theme.

The Forbidden Waters: Magic, Love, and Family Ties

By Thambo Sifiso and Khalushi Frans

Chapter 1: The Beginnings

In the village of Mangweni, life flowed with the rhythm of nature, untouched by the hands of modernity. Water was drawn from the clear, gurgling river, food was gathered from the lush forests and fertile farms, and clothing was crafted from the wool of sheep and the hides of animals. Everything about Mangweni spoke of an old-world charm. Yet, beneath its serene exterior, the village bore a dark reputation. Stories of ghosts whispered through the air, and tales of mermaids reigning in the depths of the rivers were passed down. Even more haunting were the accounts of two mysterious girls who transformed into dogs as darkness blanketed the village.

One crisp morning, the tranquillity of Mangweni was disrupted by the arrival of Frans Justin, a young man retreating from the city's unforgiving life. Once a dweller of tall skyscrapers and bustling streets, Frans returned to the rural simplicity he could now afford. He was strikingly handsome, with a tall, commanding figure, light skin that seemed to glow under the sun, and teeth as white as pearls. His deep voice resonated like a distant thunder, captivating everyone who heard him. The villagers, intrigued by his city-bred allure, couldn't help but steal glances at the newcomer, wondering about his past and purpose.

As Frans explored the village, he was enchanted by its untamed beauty. The crisp air carried the earthy fragrance of waterfalls and fertile soil. The roaring sound of cascading water was a symphony that eased his urban-weary soul. Horses roamed freely, their presence adding to the pastoral charm, while the distant cries of wild animals hinted at nature's raw essence. The houses stood scattered, each family claiming its patch of land, their boys often relied upon for tasks like fetching wood and hunting.

Among the villagers was the Zondi family, a small household led by a widowed father and his two sons, Sifiso and Bongani. Sifiso, though short and round-bellied, possessed a sharp intellect and a curious mind. He spent his days wandering the forests, studying the stones and secrets of Mangweni. Bongani, his younger brother, was equally charming, though shorter in stature. He was devoted to their father, managing the household with care, yet carried a yearning to one day venture beyond the confines of their village and explore the world.

At the heart of the village's social life stood Mr. Mkhize's tavern, a gathering spot where villagers shared laughter, stories, and drinks. Despite the convivial atmosphere, the villagers knew to head home before nightfall, aware of the supernatural shadows lurking in Mangweni. Frans, however, remained blissfully ignorant of these warnings. For him, the tavern felt like an extension of the city's nightlife. He indulged in alcohol, oblivious to the dangers that prowled under the veil of darkness.

Mr. Mkhize had a family of his own—a wife and two daughters, Sibongile and Zandile. These sisters were as enchanting as they were mysterious, their beauty almost otherworldly. Their smooth black skin shimmered under the sun, their long hair cascading like rivers of silk, and their piercing blue eyes seemed to hold secrets of another realm. Often barefoot, they moved with an ethereal grace, as if angels had descended from the heavens. Together, they fetched water from the river, where their friend Laura, the queenly mermaid, reigned supreme. Laura, both feared and revered, was said to hold dominion over the spirits of Mangweni, ensuring the village's delicate balance.

The two sisters, Sibongile and Zandile, were widely recognized in the village. At 20 and 22 years old respectively, they were celebrated for their beauty and grace. Their father, Mr. Mkhize, owned the popular tavern *eMgodini*, where the sisters often assisted in selling alcohol. Despite their frequent interactions with villagers, neither had ever been romantically involved with anyone. This left the villagers puzzled, their imaginations running wild as they speculated about the reason behind the sisters' disinterest in relationships. However, their parents remained unbothered, for they knew the dark truth: at night, their daughters transformed into wild dogs. These dogs terrorized the village, murdering unsuspecting victims and stealing from their neighbour's. After their nocturnal escapades, they would retreat to the river to meet Laura, the mermaid queen and their trusted friend.

One day, Frans, eager to learn more about the village, ventured into the forest. His steps were deliberate, his mind filled with curiosity about the land he now called home. As he explored, he unexpectedly encountered Sifiso and Bongani Zondi, who had been sent by their father to hunt. The brothers were surprised to see Frans and paused to size him up.

Frans: "Greetings, gentlemen."

Sifiso (eyeing Frans suspiciously): "Uh, greetings… What do you want?"

Frans (with a nervous smile): "I'm new to the village. I don't know anyone, and… I'd be happy if you could be my friends."

Bongani (bursts out laughing): "Friends? Look at this one, Sifiso! Did you hear that? He wants to be our *friend*! Do we look like we're running a friendship club?"

Sifiso (joining in the laughter): "Exactly! Maybe you should put up a poster— 'Seeking Friends in Mangweni.'"

Frans (a little embarrassed but persistent): "Come on, I just thought—"

Sifiso (cutting him off): "Wait, how do we even know you're real? What if you're… you know… one of *them*?"

Bongani (pretending to shiver): "Oooh, a ghost! Maybe he floats when we're not looking!"

The brothers broke into uncontrollable laughter, leaving Frans staring at them, utterly bewildered.

Frans: "What are you talking about? Ghosts?"

Sifiso (wiping tears from laughter): "Oh, don't worry about it, city boy. Just stay safe out here."

Without another word, the brothers walked off, still chuckling and leaving Frans standing there, confused and uneasy. Their words lingered in his mind: *ghost*. As he walked home, questions flooded his thoughts. Did this village truly have ghosts? The unanswered questions gnawed at him, and by the time he reached home, he had locked his doors and resolved to seek answers.

The next morning, Frans awoke early, determined to find the Zondi brothers. As he made his way through the village, he stumbled across two beautiful girls singing and playing by the roadside. Their laughter and melodious voices were enchanting, but Frans felt a chill. He paused briefly but dared not approach them. The memory of the brothers' warnings haunted him. *What if they weren't human?*

Eventually, he reached *eMgodini* and stepped into the dimly lit tavern. Behind the counter stood Mr. Mkhize, polishing a glass.

Mr. Mkhize: "Ah, young man. How can I help you?"

Frans: "Good morning, sir. I'm not here to buy anything. I'm looking for two boys—short, young, and probably carrying hunting gear."

Mr. Mkhize (nodding thoughtfully): "Ah, you must mean the Zondi boys. But who are you, and why are you looking for them?"

Frans: "I'm Frans. I met them yesterday, and… I just need to talk to them again."

Mr. Mkhize (chuckling): "Well, good luck keeping up with those two. Let me give you directions."

Following Mr. Mkhize's instructions, Frans found the brothers in a clearing, resting and chatting after a morning hunt. He approached them cautiously, tapping Sifiso on the shoulder.

Sifiso (turning abruptly): "Oh, it's you again. What do you want *this* time?"

Frans: "I couldn't sleep last night because of what you said! What did you mean by ghosts? I need answers."

Bongani (grinning mischievously): "Sit down, city boy. Let's enlighten you."

Sifiso: "This village is haunted. There's a girl who changes her name and looks beautiful, but she's not… human."

Bongani: "And there's a mermaid who lives in the river. They say she's stunning, but trust me, you don't want to meet her."

Sifiso: "And then there are the dogs. Wild beasts that roam the village at night, stealing and killing. Everyone says the village is cursed."

Frans: (wide-eyed) "Have you seen these things, or are they just stories?"

Sifiso: (nodding gravely) "We've seen the dogs. The rest? Our parents told us."

Frans: "This is… unbelievable."

Sifiso: (leaning closer) "Here's some advice—stay indoors at night. Midnight is when the real Mangweni wakes up."

Bongani: (smirking) "Now, you've got your answers. You can go."

Frans: "Wait… Can we be friends now?"

The brothers exchanged a look. Bongani burst out laughing again.

Bongani: "This one is persistent, huh? Fine. But if you slow us down, don't blame us."

Relieved, Frans followed them as they began to show him around the village. Curious about the girls he had seen earlier, he asked the brothers about them.

Frans: "By the way, who were those girls singing near the road? They were… beautiful."

Sifiso: (stopping abruptly) "Those? Oh no. Stay far away from them. They're Mr. Mkhize's daughters. Trust us, you don't want to get involved."

Bongani :(grimly) "Some beauties come with a curse, city boy. Remember that."

Chapter 2 : The Night

They went home and slept the sun rose over Mangweni, painting the skies in hues of amber and gold, as Frans stirred restlessly in his small house. His thoughts remained consumed by the beauty of the two sisters he had seen at the road, Sibongile and Zandile. Their allure had left him sleepless, and a wild idea brewed in his mind: whichever of the two crossed his path first would be the one he'd pursue.

The next morning, bleary-eyed yet determined, Frans set out to meet Sifiso and Bongani, his newfound friends. He couldn't contain his excitement as he raved about the sisters to them.

Frans (grinning): "Boys, I can't stop thinking about those two beautiful ladies! I swear, one of them is going to be mine. No, scratch that—maybe *both*!"

Sifiso (laughing, shaking his head): "Eish, my friend, we also wanted them once, but not even a single glance in our direction. Those two? Impossible."

Bongani (teasing): "But hey, good luck! You'll need it, city boy."

Frans (leaning forward confidently): "Luck? Let's make this interesting. I'll bet you—by the end of this, I'll get one of them. Maybe even both!"

Both Sifiso and Bongani erupted in laughter, clutching their stomachs.

Sifiso (wiping a tear from his eye): "You? You think you're some kind of Romeo? We'll see, Frans. We'll see."

The trio continued their hunting, the mood light with playful banter. As the sun began to dip below the horizon, Bongani suggested they go fishing the next day, an idea met with unanimous excitement.

(As they packed up for the day, Frans, his spirits high, suggested a stop at the tavern.)

Frans: "Come on, guys, let's grab a drink or two before heading home."

Bongani (glancing at the sky): "No way, Frans. Look at the time! Let's just go home."

Sifiso (nodding): "Yeah, you go if you want, but don't say we didn't warn you."

Unbothered, Frans parted ways with them and headed to the tavern alone, unaware of the danger that awaited. He entered, his eyes scanning the room for the sisters, but to his disappointment, they were nowhere in sight.

Frans (to Mr. Mkhize): "Evening, sir. Can I have a beer?"

Mr. Mkhize: "Sure thing, young man. That'll be R20."

Frans paid and settled into his seat, waiting and drinking. One beer turned into several, and as his money flowed freely, Mr. Mkhize couldn't help but notice. Sensing an opportunity, he quietly called his daughters.

Mr. Mkhize (whispering to the sisters): "Girls, that young man has money. Follow him when he leaves. You know what to do."

The sisters nodded but exchanged uncertain glances.

Frans finally stumbled out of the tavern, the alcohol clouding his senses. As he tried to navigate the dark path home, he felt a strange presence. Behind him, the sisters had transformed into wild dogs and were following him. But as they drew closer, Zandile hesitated.

Zandile (whispering): "Sibongile, I can't attack him. He's… too handsome."

Sibongile (frowning): "What? Because he's handsome? Are you serious?"

Zandile: "Yes, sis. I like him. Let's spare him, please."

Sibongile (sighing): "Fine. But what do we tell Baba?"

Zandile: "We'll say he outsmarted us and ran away. That should work."

Sibongile: "Alright. But what do we do with the rest of the night?"

Zandile (grinning): "The usual, of course."

Meanwhile, Frans staggered down the path, his mind spinning. Suddenly, he saw a woman emerge from the shadows. She was breathtakingly beautiful—tall, dark-skinned, with eyes that seemed to pierce his soul. Her lips were full, her teeth dazzlingly white, and her voice smooth as silk.

Neira: "How can such a handsome man struggle alone in the dark?"

Frans (rubbing his eyes): "Struggle? No, I'm not struggling. I'm just… distracted. By your beauty."

Neira: (smiling coyly): "Are you sure about that?"

Frans: "Absolutely. I've never seen anyone as stunning as you. Everyone else I've met is nothing compared to you."

She stepped closer, her dress clinging to her figure.

Neira: "Would you like to see more of this?"

Frans (grinning): "Yes! I'd be the happiest man alive."

She introduced herself as Naira and led Frans to her house. Once inside, she poured him more alcohol, and they quickly became intimate. Frans, drunk and captivated, fell asleep beside her, a satisfied smile on his face.

When he awoke the next morning, the world around him was unrecognizable. Instead of Naira's cozy house, he found himself lying naked in a graveyard. Panic surged through him as he turned to his right and saw a tombstone that read: *Naira Meia, born 1926, Died 1956.*

Frans (screaming): "No! No, no, no!"

He scrambled to his feet and saw bones beside him, half-covered by a white cloth. Without another thought, he bolted, running home as fast as his legs could carry him, his screams echoing through the village.

When he finally reached his house, Sifiso and Bongani were waiting for him.

Sifiso: "Frans! What happened? We've been worried."

Frans (sobbing): "I… I slept with a ghost. She was so beautiful, but she… she's dead!"

Sifiso (shaking his head): "We warned you, Frans. This village is dangerous. You're lucky you weren't eaten by the dogs."

Bongani: "But now what? What happens when you sleep with a ghost?"

Sifiso: "They say it's bad luck. If you don't fix it, you could die within a week."

Chapter 3 : Paying of the sins

The trio decided to consult Bongani's father, Mr. Zondi, who listened intently to Frans' story.

Mr. Zondi: "This is serious. You must go to the Nkomazi River with a goat and some coins. Offer them to the queen of the river, and she may forgive you. If she gives you something in return, you're safe. If not, well… prepare for the worst."

Following his advice, the boys prepared for the journey. Frans and his friends, Sifiso and Bongani, walked quietly toward the river, their footsteps crunching against the dry earth beneath them. Along the way, they heard soft, melodious singing. Curious, they edged closer to the source of the sound and discovered the Mkhize sisters, Sibongile and Zandile, half-naked and singing as they bathed under the moonlight.

Bongani: (*whispering with a mischievous grin*) "Look who we've stumbled upon. It's the Mkhize angels."

Sifiso: (*shaking his head firmly*) "Focus, Bongani. We have a mission, and it's not chasing girls."

Frans: (*staring for a moment longer before sighing*) "Let's go. The river won't wait for us."

They continued toward the river, pushing thoughts of the enchanting sisters aside to concentrate on the task at hand. Once they reached the riverbank, they found a stick to draw out their plan in the sand and began preparing the boat.

Frans: (*grinning at Sifiso*) "My friend, you know this place better than I do. Please, guide me, and I'll follow."

Sifiso: (*nodding with a serious expression*) "We'll follow the map and use the wind. If it pulls us in the right direction, we'll know when we've reached the middle of the river."

Bongani: (*leaning in with a teasing smirk*) "And Frans, you need to call your name—loudly. Inform the queen that we're coming. She deserves a grand announcement."

They laughed nervously, but their determination was unwavering. They climbed into the boat, began rowing, and sang songs as they threw coins into the water. The melody echoed eerily in the still night, blending with the sound of the river's gentle current.

As the day gave way to night, they reached the middle of the river. Frans threw coins into the water until the river turned red.

Sifiso:(*staring in shock*)"The water—it's red! Is this supposed to happen?"

Bongani:(*his voice trembling*) "We knew something would happen, but I didn't expect this."

Frans: (*taking a deep breath*) "Stay calm." *He reached for the goat they had brought and threw it into the water.*

The goat disappeared beneath the surface, and the water returned to its serene blue. Moments later, a box emerged, floating gently toward their boat. Frans grabbed it with shaking hands, his heart pounding. They started their journey home, singing softly, their voices laced with a mix of relief and exhaustion.

By the time they reached the village, dawn had broken. Sifiso and Bongani, too tired to continue, went to their homes to rest, leaving Frans to carry the mysterious box back to his house.

Once inside, Frans placed the box on his bed, his curiosity burning. He stepped into the shower to wash away the river's chill, but his mind was consumed by thoughts of the box. Dripping wet and half-naked, he decided he couldn't wait any longer. He opened the box.

(From within, a radiant light filled the room, and a young woman with long, fair, jet-black hair appeared. Her beauty was otherworldly, and Frans stumbled back in shock.)

Laura: *(her voice smooth like flowing water)* "Why are you scared?"

Frans: *(stammering), his voice shaking* "Who... who are you?"

Laura: *(smiling faintly)* "I am Laura, the queen of the river. You went there to appease me, did you not?"

Frans: *(his heart racing)* "What do you want from me?"

Laura: *(stepping closer, her gaze piercing)* "Didn't they tell you? To wipe away your sins, you must sleep with me. Only then will you be forgiven."

Frans: *(retreating to the corner of the room)* "But... I'm scared. What if I break some rule?"

Laura: *(her tone firm, unyielding)* "You must choose—life or death."

Overcome by fear and allure, Frans gave in. The night was filled with passion, and by morning, Laura disappeared, leaving behind a small bag filled with gold coins—a sign of her satisfaction. Frans, now forgiven, slept peacefully for the first time in months.

Chapter 4: The dogs

The following day, Frans woke with renewed energy. He shared his happiness with Sifiso and Bongani, who agreed to celebrate with him. They went to Mr. Mkhize's tavern, where, to Frans' delight, Zandile and Sibongile were assisting their parents.

Frans: *grinning as he approached Zandile* "Hi there, beautiful lady. Can I get your service?"

Zandile: *glancing at him with a polite smile* "Yes. What can I get you?"

Frans: *(leaning closer)* "I heard your name is Zandile. Is that right?"

Zandile: (*nodding cautiously*) "Yes, it is. How can I help you?"

Frans: (*grinning sheepishly*) "Can I... can I have you?"

Zandile: (*frowning*), taken aback "Excuse me?"

Frans: (*laughing nervously*) "I mean, can I get to know you?"

Zandile: (*shaking her head with a smirk*) "My parents would never allow that. Now, what can I get you?"

Frans: (*sighing*) "Fine, just the alcohol."

(*Zandile handed over the alcohol while Sifiso and Bongani burst out laughing.*)

Sifiso: (*mocking Frans with a grin*) "I told you to stay away from those girls, but you never listen!"

Their laughter echoed as the night deepened. But while Sifiso and Bongani joked, Frans couldn't stop thinking about Zandile's beauty. Even in his sleep, she dominated his dreams.

The next day, Frans returned to the river, hoping to see Zandile again. As fate would have it, Zandile had been sent to fetch water alone. Frans heard her singing as he approached.

Frans: (*joining her song with a wide grin*) "You have such a beautiful voice."

Zandile: (*blushing lightly*) "Thank you. But I must hurry home."

Frans: (*stepping closer*) "Let me help you."

Zandile: (*smiling softly*) "That won't be necessary."

Frans: (*earnestly*) "I want to know you better."

Zandile: (*hesitating, then smiling shyly*) "You're very handsome. Who could refuse to be known by you?"

Frans: (*his voice gentle*) "It's an honor to hear that."

(*They walked back to the Mkhize house together, chatting along the way. At the door, Mrs. Mkhize stood waiting, her arms crossed.*)

Mrs. Mkhize: (*sternly*) "Zandile, who is this?"

Zandile: (*glancing nervously at Frans*) "It's Frans, Mama."

Frans: (*nervously smiling*) "Hi, Mama."

Mrs. Mkhize: (*glaring*) "I'm not your mother. I'm warning you, boy, stay away from my daughter!"

While Zandile was speaking to her mother, Sibongile and Frans found themselves standing together, exchanging words, their conversation growing more intimate by the minute. Zandile, noticing the spark between them, couldn't hold back her discomfort.

Frans: (grinning) "You know, Zandile, I don't think I've ever met anyone quite like you."

Zandile: (shyly) "Well, that's good to hear… but, you should really get going. My mom won't like it if you're here too long."

Frans: "Why so soon? I thought we were just getting started."

Zandile: (glancing nervously at her mother) "Please, just go. I can't have you here any longer."

Mrs. Mkhize: (sternly) "That's enough. He needs to leave. Now."

Frans, a little taken aback, flashed Zandile one last smile before turning to leave. His head was full of her—her smile, her eyes, the way she spoke so softly yet made him feel like the only person in the world. He couldn't shake the thoughts of her, even as he returned to his home and tried to fall asleep.

But sleep didn't come easily. The next morning, the pull of the river, and of Zandile, was too strong. He had to see her again. As he approached the river, he spotted her standing there, waiting as if she had expected him all along.

Frans: (grinning) "I knew you'd be here."

Zandile: (laughing) "You couldn't stay away, could you?"

Frans: (teasing) "Maybe I couldn't. You've got a way of keeping me coming back."

Without another word, they began splashing each other with water, laughing like carefree children. The air between them was electric, charged with an unspoken connection. As the water soaked through their clothes, something shifted—Zandile, unable to contain herself, began to undress, leaving herself completely exposed.

Frans, his heart racing, followed her lead, stripping down. They stood there, exposed and vulnerable, caught up in the moment. But just as their hands reached for each other, a voice rang out.

Mrs. Mkhize: (furious, brandishing a *syambok*) "ZANDILE! What are you doing?!"

(Zandile froze, fear flashing across her face. Frans, caught in the act, turned pale, his body stiff with shock.)

Zandile: (flustered) "Mom, I... I'm sorry."

Mrs. Mkhize: (seething with anger) "You, Frans—get out of here! If I ever see you near my daughter again, I will make sure you regret it. You hear me? Ask around. People know what I'm capable of!"

Frans, his stomach in knots, quickly dressed and fled the scene. His mind was reeling, and he couldn't stop thinking about Zandile and her mother's words. On his way back to the village, he bumped into Sibongile, who had been sent to fetch water since Zandile was grounded.

Sibongile: (smiling slyly) "Frans, I'm glad I caught you."

Frans: (still shaken) "What's up, Sibongile?"

Sibongile: (looking at him with a twinkle in her eye) "I've been thinking... You don't belong with Zandile."

Frans: (confused) "What do you mean?"

Sibongile: (leaning in, lowering her voice) "I'm the firstborn, Frans. I'm the one who's meant to be with you. Zandile... she's not the one for you. You and I... we were made for each other."

Frans felt his heart race. He didn't know what to make of her words, but there was something undeniable about the way Sibongile spoke to him—something that made him want to believe her.

Frans: (hesitant) "But... Zandile... she's different. She's special."

Sibongile: (softly, confidently) "I understand, but sometimes the things we think we want aren't really what we need. Don't you see? You and I, we fit. I'm the one who can make you happy."

Her words were like a spell, and before he could stop himself, he felt himself drawn to her. Sibongile took a step closer, her gaze fixed on him with an intensity he couldn't ignore. With a slow, deliberate motion, she began to undress, her actions speaking volumes.

Frans: (almost breathless) "Sibongile... what are you doing?"

Sibongile: (with a teasing smile) "What do you think I'm doing?"

The air around them seemed to thicken, charged with desire and temptation. Frans, unable to resist, watched as Sibongile slowly removed her clothes, revealing her vulnerability. The moment was electric, and everything else seemed to fade into the background

Sibongile, her eyes locked onto Frans, took a step forward, her voice lowering to a whisper.

Sibongile: (with an enticing smile) "Frans... don't hold back. Let go. We both know what we want."

Mrs. Mkhize: (shouting from a distance) "Sibongile! What is this nonsense?!"

Sibongile froze in shock, her breath caught in her throat. The moment was shattered. Before anyone could move, Mrs. Mkhize stormed in, her eyes blazing with fury. Frans, terrified, quickly scrambled to his feet, dressing as fast as he could.

Mrs. Mkhize: (seething, eyes narrowing) "What do you think you're doing, Sibongile? You know better than this. I won't let you ruin everything."

Sibongile: (stammering) "Mom, I... I didn't mean—"

Mrs. Mkhize: (cutting her off) "Enough! You're coming with me. You and your sister will take care of this. It's the only way."

Sibongile, shaken but resolute, nodded, her eyes betraying the fear and confusion swirling in her mind. Mrs. Mkhize turned to her with a menacing glare.

Mrs. Mkhize: (coldly) "Frans has crossed a line. He needs to pay for this."

Meanwhile, Frans, oblivious to what was unfolding behind him, started his walk home. The air felt unusually heavy, and he couldn't shake the feeling that something was terribly wrong. His steps quickened, his thoughts clouded by the events of the past few hours. But before he could get too far, the chilling sound of footsteps behind him caught his attention.

He turned to find two massive, vicious dogs emerging from the shadows, their eyes glowing with malice. The dogs growled, their teeth bared, and their approach was swift and determined. Frans' heart raced, his breaths shallow and panicked. He turned to run, but the ground beneath him was uneven, and he stumbled, falling hard.

The dogs were upon him in an instant, their snarling jaws inches from his throat. He could feel their hot breath on his skin, the sharpness of their teeth just moments away from sinking into him. His hands scrambled against the dirt, desperately trying to push himself up.

Just as he thought it was over, a rope flew through the air and landed with a crack near the dogs' necks. Mr. Zondo, with a swift and practiced motion, pulled the rope tight, forcing the dogs back. The animals whined and growled, but they were contained.

Mr. Zondo: (with a stern, commanding voice) "Get up, Frans. You're not done yet."

Frans, breathing heavily, tried to stand, his legs shaking from the adrenaline. Before he could speak, Mrs. Mkhize appeared, her expression one of icy rage. She stared at him, her eyes dark with fury.

Mrs. Mkhize: (coldly) "You're lucky, Frans. This time. But don't think you're free. If I see you near my daughter again, I will make sure it's the last time you ever see the light of day."

Frans, his heart still racing, didn't wait to respond. He bolted away, running as fast as he could, not daring to look back. He could feel Mrs. Mkhize's gaze on him even as he disappeared into the distance. The threat hung over him like a shadow, and he knew, deep down, that he had only narrowly escaped.

Mr. Zondi, watching Frans with concern, saw the signs of his life spiraling out of control. The young man seemed trapped in a cycle of poor decisions, and Mr. Zondi feared that if Frans continued down this path, it would only be a matter of time before something terrible happened. So, he made a decision—to adopt Frans and give him a chance at a better life, far from the chaos that surrounded him.

Chapter 5 : The legacy of the river

One afternoon, **Frans, Sifiso, and Bongani** decided to go camping by the river, hoping to escape the madness of their everyday lives. The promise of fishing, storytelling, and spending time by the water made the trip irresistible. They packed up their boat and set out to the riverside, each of them excited about the adventure that awaited.

They set up camp by the river and began fishing. The quiet of nature enveloped them, and the sound of the river's current mixed with the occasional laughter from the boys as they fished. They managed to catch a few fish, their bounty for the night's meal, but little did they know that something far more extraordinary was about to unfold.

As they fished, they noticed something unusual—**a lady**, lying motionless on a wooden board in the river. The sight startled them, but they didn't hesitate.

Frans: (concerned) "Guys, do you see that? Someone's in trouble!"

Sifiso: (squinting) "It looks like a woman. We need to help her."

Without thinking twice, the three friends rowed their boat towards the lady, pulling her gently into their vessel. She was pale, shivering, and cold to the touch, wrapped in a thin cloth. They covered her with a thicker blanket they had on board and made sure she was warm. But the funny part is that Frans could not see that the Laura that once visited him is the same Laura.

The woman slowly stirred as they rowed back to their campsite, and as the boat reached the shore, she spoke in a soft, melodic voice.

Lady (Laura): (weakly) "Thank you... thank you for saving me."

She was still shaking, but her presence was calming, almost ethereal. They made a fire, and **Laura**, as she introduced herself, prepared a warm meal of soup for them. The boys watched her closely, amazed by her kindness and the way she cared for them as if she'd known them for years.

That evening, after a hearty meal, they all sat around the fire, chatting and enjoying the peace of the night. Laura shared a story about how she had ended up in the river.

Laura: (smiling gently) "I was separated from my family many years ago... I fell into the river while looking for herbs. I've been here ever since, watching over the waters."

Her story was convincing, though there was something in her eyes—something deep and ancient—that made the boys question just how true her tale was. But they were too caught up in the moment to worry. Laura felt like a sister to them, and they welcomed her into their circle.

The next day, Laura assisted the boys in climbing a tree to fetch coconuts, all the while sharing tales of the river's mysteries. The boys had never met anyone like her before—her charm, her grace, and the mysterious aura she carried around her made her seem almost otherworldly. She even helped them build their camp, showing them tricks of the trade they hadn't known before.

At night, after a long day of fishing, climbing, and chatting, they settled down around the fire. Laura cooked a delicious meal that tasted unlike anything the boys had ever had before—rich and savory, with spices that seemed to come from another world.

Bongani: (taking a bite) "This is incredible, Laura. What's your secret?"

Laura: (laughing softly) "It's just something I learned from the river. It gives me the strength to cook for those who need it."

The night passed in blissful harmony. They laughed, played, and shared stories. But as the boys slept soundly in their tents, Laura quietly slipped away into the river. She had something important to do.

As they woke up the next morning, they noticed something startling—**a box** of gold, diamonds, silver, and coins had appeared at the edge of their camp. The boys stood in awe, their eyes wide with disbelief. The treasure glittered under the morning sun, more than they had ever dreamed of.

Frans: (stunned) "Where did this come from?"

Sifiso: (wide-eyed) "This can't be real... can it?"

They looked around, expecting to see Laura, but she was gone. Only the gentle ripples in the river betrayed her departure. When they looked across the river, they saw her wave from a distance before disappearing into the mist, leaving them speechless.

Bongani: (whispering) "Did she leave us this...?"

Before they could speak more about it, the girls from the Mkhize family, Zandile and Sibongile, who had caused so much trouble in the village, were found dead. It was said that **the Queen of the River**, Laura herself, had taken action against them for their evil ways. The village was shaken, but many felt a sense of relief as the girls' spirits were put to rest.

As for the Zondi family, the riches they had received from Laura transformed their lives forever. With the treasure, they built a legacy, becoming wealthy and respected in the village. They never spoke of the events at the river again, but they always remembered the kind woman who had saved them from the depths of despair.

And **Laura**, the mermaid, remained the queen of the river, her story intertwined with the lives of the boys who had once been her saviours. As for Frans, he realized that sometimes the river doesn't just give—it takes, and its gifts are never without a price.

www.ingramcontent.com/pod-product-compliance
Lightning Source LLC
Chambersburg PA
CBHW071439220526
45469CB00004B/1599